WAR MACHINES
WARPLANES

Simon Adams

IN ASSOCIATION WITH

IMPERIAL WAR
MUSEUM

Smart Apple Media is published by Black Rabbit Books
P.O. Box 3263, Mankato, Minnesota 56002

Printed in the United States

Published by arrangement with the Watts Publishing Group Ltd, London.

Library of Congress Cataloging-in-Publication Data
Adams, Simon, 1955–
    Warplanes / Simon Adams.
    p. cm.—(Smart Apple Media. War machines)
    Summary: "Describes several models of military aircraft used in World War I and World War II, including
    specifications and statistics"—Provided by publisher.
    Includes index.
    ISBN 978-1-59920-223-5
    1. Airplanes, Military—History—20th century—Juvenile literature. 2. World War, 1914–1918—Aerial
    operations—Juvenile literature. 3. World War, 1939–1945—Aerial operations—Juvenile literature. I. Title.
UG1240.A36 2009
623.74'6-dc22
                                                                                          2007039964

Editor: Sarah Ridley
Editor-in-chief: John C. Miles
Designer: Jason Billin
Art director: Jonathan Hair

Picture credits
Cover main Wikimedia Commons: Chowells

All other images copyright © Imperial War Museum. Cover bottom left ZZZ4727E, bottom middle Q63847,
bottom right NYP65472; Title page Q67902; page 4 Q63847; page 5 CH2926; page 6 Q68124; page 7
Q57615A; page 8 Q67902; page 9 Q20641; page 10 Q63786; page 11 Q63784; page 12 Q63847; page 13
top Q44797, bottom Q50329; page 14 Q63778; page 15 Q63779; page 16 Q67573; page 17 Q67328; page
18 HU44156; page 19 MH6665; page 20 EA74532; page 21 top AP12412, bottom EA19178; page 22 CH2926;
page 23 CH5249; page 24 OEM 3647; page 25 ZZZ5806E; page 26 CH6299; page 27 left NYP65472, right
EH18955; page 28 HU95885; HU95886; page 30 background Q63779.

9 8 7 6 5 4 3 2

Contents

Introduction

On December 17, 1903, the Wright brothers took to the skies in their aircraft named Flyer at Kitty Hawk, North Carolina. Their short flight was the first controlled, powered aircraft flight in human history.

World War I

Early aircraft were small, flimsy machines, carrying only the pilot and perhaps one crew member. But a little over ten years later, in 1914, World War I broke out in Europe. Aircraft now became weapons of war. The fighters were equipped with machine guns to attack each other in the skies, while some larger aircraft had enough space to carry bombs to drop on enemy territory. By the end of the war in 1918, aircraft were large and powerful enough to fly much longer distances.

World War II

Twenty years later, in 1939, World War II broke out. The new fighter aircraft were small and fast, while massive, slow-moving bombers carried a huge weight of bombs to rain down on enemy towns and cities.

All 12 aircraft in this book flew during these two world wars. Each one has an interesting story to tell, and all of them show how rapidly aircraft developed from that first day in North Carolina when powered flight began.

ROYAL AIRCRAFT FACTORY
BE2

The British Royal Aircraft Factory BE2 first flew in February 1912 and entered combat in 1914 as a reconnaissance (observation) aircraft.

However, it was slow and hard to maneuver, making it an easy target for German fighter planes. From 1917 onward, a later version was used only for home defense and for training new pilots.

Airship Shot Down

In one brief moment of fame, on the night of September 2, 1916, a BE2 shot down the first German airship over Britain. The pilot, Captain William Leefe-Robinson, was awarded the Victoria Cross for his brave attack on the airship.

▼ The BE2 was a flimsy, underpowered airplane and was easily attacked by German fighters.

★ The BE stands for Blériot Experimental, named after Louis Blériot, the French pilot who made the first flight across the English Channel on July 25, 1909.

★ The second crew member, the observer, was armed only with a rifle in the first models of the BE2. In the BE2c, a machine gun was provided for his use.

PERFORMANCE

Maximum speed	75 mph (120 km/h)
Range	200 miles (320 km)
Service ceiling	10,000 ft (3,048 m)

▼ *A biplane has two parallel wings, usually supported by solid struts and wire rope.*

SPECS & STATS

Crew	Two—pilot and observer
Height	11 ft 1 in (3.4 m)
Loaded weight	2,142 lb (972 kg)
Armament	One .303-caliber (7.7-mm) Lewis machine gun Two 112-lb (51-kg) or ten 20-lb (9-kg) bombs
Engine	One Royal Aircraft Factory 1a, 90 hp engine

Span	37 ft (11.28 m)
Length	27 ft 3 in (8.31 m)

SOPWITH
CAMEL

The Sopwith Camel was one of the main British fighter planes during the later years of World War I.

The Camel first flew in December 1916. More than 5,500 were produced before the war ended in November 1918.

A Challenge to Fly

The Camel could make some clever moves but was not easy to fly. Engine, pilot, guns, and fuel tank were all placed in the first 7 ft (2 m) of the aircraft, which made it difficult to handle. In addition, the Clerget engine needed exactly the right fuel mixture. Otherwise, it failed during take off. Despite these problems, the Camel was successful in combat, shooting down 1,294 German aircraft.

▼ *The short, stubby Camel.*

Its powerful engine allowed the Camel to take off from the short runway deck of HMS Pegasus.

★ The Camel got its name because of the hump surrounding the gun installation in front of the pilot.

★ The two forward-firing Vickers guns were synchronized to fire through the spinning propellers without hitting them.

PERFORMANCE

Maximum speed	115 mph (185 km/h)
Range	300 miles (485 km)
Service ceiling	21,100 ft (6,400 m)

SPECS & STATS

Crew	One—pilot	**Span**	28 ft (8.53 m)
Height	8 ft 6 in (2.59 m)	**Length**	18 ft 9 in (5.71 m)
Loaded weight	1,455 lb (660 kg)		
Armament	Two .303-caliber (7.7 -mm) Vickers machine guns		
Engine	One Clerget 9B, 9-cylinder, 130 hp rotary engine		

Gotha G.V

▼ *The Gotha G.V was an extremely effective bomber.*

The Gotha G.V was the fifth in a series of heavy bombers used by the German air service during World War I.

The Germans first used vast Zeppelin airships to drop bombs on London and other targets in southeast England. However, the airships were too slow and easy to hit, so they were replaced in the summer of 1917 by the Gotha bombers.

FACT FILE

★ The Gotha began life as a large, twin-engine seaplane that was adapted to become a land-based bomber by its designer, Oskar Ursinus, when he was conscripted into the German army in 1914.

★ An opening in the underside of the fuselage allowed the rear gunner to fire at targets below and behind the bomber.

Royal Air Force Begins

The Gotha bombers caused great alarm, because the British had few aircraft in 1917 able to catch the Gothas and prevent them from attacking. The British therefore reorganized their air defenses, creating the Royal Air Force (RAF), the world's first independent air force, on April 1, 1918.

▼ *Its 77 ft 9 In (23.7 m) wingspan made the Gotha G.V instantly recognizable from the ground.*

PERFORMANCE

Maximum speed	87 mph (140 km/h)
Range	520 miles (840 km)
Service ceiling	21,300 ft (6,500 m)

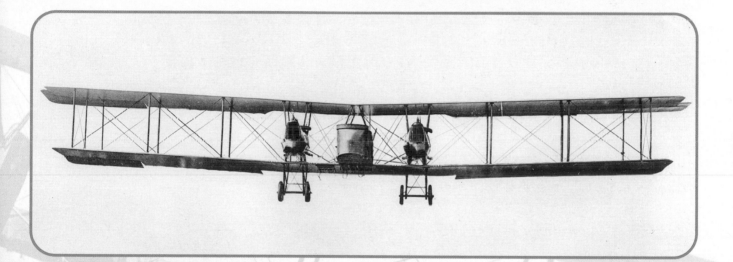

SPECS & STATS

Crew	Three—pilot, gunner, and bombadier (rear gunner)
Span	77 ft 9 in (23.7 m) **Height** 14 ft (4.5 m)
Length	12.42 m (40 ft 9 in)
Loaded weight	8,745 lb (3,967 kg)
Armament	Two or three .31-caliber (7.92-mm) Parabellum LMG 14 machine guns 1,102-lb (500-kg) bombs
Engines	Two Mercedes D.IVa inline, 260 hp engines

Fokker
Dr.1 Triplane

The German Fokker triplane made its appearance over the battlefields of Western Europe in August 1917.

The new aircraft was very maneuverable, but it was much slower than many fighter planes of the Allies and difficult to land.

The "Red Baron"

The most famous pilot to fly a Fokker Dr.1 was Baron Manfred von Richthofen, the "Red Baron." The legendary air ace made his name when he painted his Albatros D.111 fighter bright red. He shot down 80 enemy aircraft before he himself was shot down and killed on April 21, 1918.

PERFORMANCE

Maximum speed	105 mph (185 km/h)
Range	185 miles (300 km)
Service ceiling	20,000 ft (6,095 m)

▲ The Dr.1 was short and stubby but very maneuverable in the air.

★ The Dr. in the name stands for *Dreidecker*, the German word for a triplane.

★ The photo on the right shows part of the wall in von Richthofen's quarters. Displayed are numbers taken from enemy aircraft shot down by him.

The Germans often painted faces on the front of their airplanes.

SPECS & STATS

Crew	One—pilot	**Span**	23 ft 7 in (7.2 m)
Height	9 ft 8 in (2.95 m)	**Length**	18 ft 11 in (5.77 m)
Loaded weight	1,292 lb (586 kg)		
Armament	Two .31 caliber (7.92 mm) LMG 08/15 Spandau machine guns		
Engine	One Oberursel UR.II, 9-cylinder, 110 hp rotary engine		

Fokker D.VII

The German Fokker D.VII fighter only made its appearance at the very end of World War I, but it quickly proved to be the best fighter in the sky.

It could dive and climb with ease and easily outmaneuvered many enemy aircraft.

Fearsome Fighter

Indeed, the Fokker was so feared by Britain and France that it was the only aircraft to be mentioned in the armistice (cease-fire) agreements that ended the war with Germany in November 1918. The Germans were told to "surrender in good condition... all aircraft of the D.VII type."

▼ *The crosses on the fuselage, tail, and wings identify this as a German airplane.*

FOKKER BIPLANE.

▼ *The Fokker D.VII was easily the best fighter of the war.*

Maximum speed	116 mph (186 km/h)
Range	170 miles (273 km)
Service ceiling	19,600 ft (5,970 m)

FACT FILE

★ Many D.VIIs were covered with linen printed in irregular colored shapes. These shapes merged together at a distance to form an effective camouflage.

★ The use of printed fabric rather than paint reduced the body weight of the aircraft.

SPECS & STATS

Crew	One—pilot	**Span**	29 ft 3 in (8.93 m)
Height	9 ft 2 in (2.8 m)	**Length**	22 ft 9 in (6.93 m)
Loaded weight	1,874 lb (850 kg)		
Armament	Two .31-caliber (7.92-mm) LMG 08/15 Spandau machine guns		
Engine	One Mercedes D111a, 180 hp engine		

Vickers
Vimy FB 27A

The British Vickers Vimy entered service in October 1918, at the very end of World War I, and so played no part in the conflict.

However, it served successfully as the main heavy bomber of the British RAF throughout the 1920s.

Transatlantic First

The aircraft does have one massive claim to fame, however. In June 1919, Captain John Alcock and Lieutenant Arthur Brown flew a modified Vickers Vimy nonstop across the Atlantic Ocean from Newfoundland in Canada to Connemara in Ireland, the first time this had been achieved. The aircraft flew through so much snow and ice that Brown had to continually climb onto the wings to remove ice from the air intakes of the engines.

▼ *The Vickers Vimy was an effective bomber and a good long-distance aircraft.*

PERFORMANCE

Maximum speed	100 mph (165 km/h)
Range	900 miles (1,448 km)
Service ceiling	7,000 ft (2,135 m)

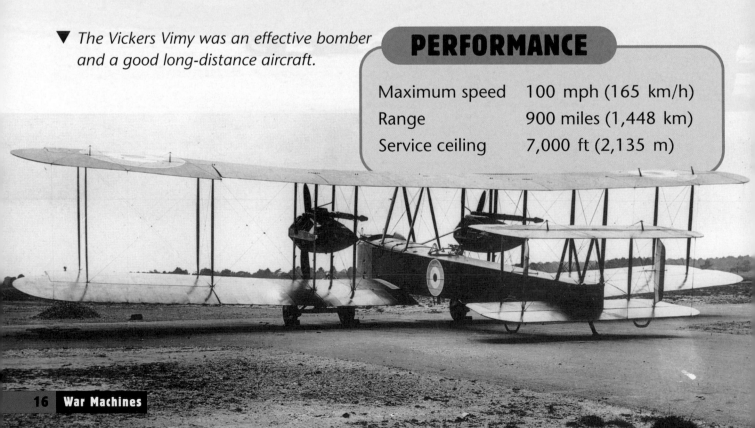

FACT FILE

★ The first Vickers Vimy flew on November 30, 1917. It was named after the Battle of Vimy Ridge, during which Canadian troops captured the ridge in eastern France from the Germans in April 1917.

★ The Vimy was a very versatile aircraft. Versions were made for civilian use, to transport military equipment, and as an air ambulance to carry wounded servicemen to hospitals.

▲ Early versions of the Vickers Vimy had Fiat rather than Rolls-Royce engines.

SPECS & STATS

Crew	Three—pilot, front gunner, and bombadier (rear gunner)
Span	68 ft 1 in (20.75 m) **Height** 15 ft 8 in (4.76 m)
Length	43 ft 7 in (13.27 m)
Loaded weight	10,884 lb (4,937 kg)
Armament	Two .303-caliber (7.7 -mm) Lewis machine guns 2,476 lb (1,123 kg) bombs
Engines	Two Rolls-Royce Eagle VIII, 360 hp engines

Messerschmitt Bf 109

The Messerschmitt Bf 109 was one of the first modern fighters of World War II. It included such features as an enclosed cockpit and retractable landing gear.

It also used the revolutionary new *monocoque* construction that did away with internal frameworks and carried the weight of the plane in its all-metal skin.

Germany's Workhorse

First flown on May 28, 1935, the Bf 109 was the standard fighter of the Luftwaffe in World War II. It served in escort, interceptor, ground-attack, and reconnaissance roles. More than 31,000 were built before the end of World War II, more than any other fighter aircraft in history. There were many models. The BF 109E was prominent when World War II began.

▼ *The retractable wheels helped to make the Messerschmitt aerodynamic in flight.*

★ The "Bf" of the aircraft's name referred to the Bayerische Flugzeuwerke (Bavarian Aircraft Works) company that designed it. When the chief designer, Willy Messerschmitt, took over the company and renamed it in 1938, the aircraft became known as the Me 109, although the old name remained in frequent use.

★ The "E" version was called Emil. All the Bf models had personal names: A for Anton, B for Bruno, C for Caesar, D for Dora, and so on.

The controls might look complex, but the plane was in fact quite easy to fly.

PERFORMANCE

Maximum speed	354 mph (570 km/h) at 20,677 ft (6,300 m)
Range	412 miles (663 km)
Service ceiling	36,091 ft (11,000 m)

SPECS & STATS

Crew	One—pilot	**Span**	32 ft 4 in (9.85 m)
Height	11 ft 2 in (3.4 m)	**Length**	28 ft 4 in (8.63 m)
Loaded weight	5,523 lb (2,505 kg)		
Armament	Two .31-caliber (7.92-mm) MG 17 machine guns above the engine Two MG FF/M cannons in the wings		
Engine	One Daimler-Benz DB 601A–1, liquid-cooled, inverted V–12, 1,100 hp engine		

Boeing B-17 Flying Fortress

▲ *Many Flying Fortresses were left unpainted.*

The American Boeing B-17 Flying Fortress is one of the most famous aircraft ever built. The B–17 prototype first flew on July 28, 1935.

A reporter for the *Seattle Times* saw the plane and nicknamed it the "Flying Fortress," because it had so many guns. Boeing quickly saw the value of this new name and trademarked it for use.

The aircraft served in every World War II combat zone, but is best known for the daylight bombing of Germany. Production ended in May 1945 and totaled 12,731.

PERFORMANCE

Maximum speed	287 mph (462 km/h)
Cruising speed	182 mph (293 km/h)
Range	2,000 miles (3,219 km)
Service ceiling	35,600 ft (10,850 m)

> ▶ Armored "flak jackets" saved the lives of many gun-turret crew members.

SPECS & STATS

Crew	Ten—pilot, co-pilot, navigator, bombardier/nose-gunner, flight-engineer/top-turret gunner, radio operator, two waist gunners, ball-turret gunner, tail gunner
Span	103 ft 9 in (31.62 m)
Height	19 ft 1 in (5.82 m)
Length	74 ft 4 in (22.66 m)
Loaded weight	72,000 lb (32,659 kg)
Armament	Thirteen .50 caliber (12.7 mm) M2 Browning machine guns 8,000 lb (3,600 kg) bombs on short-range missions, up to 400 miles (640 km) 4,500 lb (2,000 kg) bombs on long-range missions, up to 800 miles (1,280 km)
Engines	Four Wright R-1820-97 Cyclone, turbo-supercharged, radial 1,200 hp engines

Ground crewmen load a bomb on a B-17 they hope will make a direct hit.

SPECIAL EASTER EGG FOR "HITLER"

FACT FILE

★ The ball-turret gunner had to stay in position throughout a flight— no rest stops for him!

★ The B–17 flew during daylight and was open to enemy attack. It needed an escort of fighter planes.

Supermarine
Spitfire

The British single-seat Spitfire was probably the most famous fighter of all during World War II.

It was also the only fighter that was in continual production before, during, and after the war.

The Battle of Britain

In 1940, when Britain was under attack from the German Luftwaffe, Spitfire pilots took to the skies every day to protect Britain from aerial attack. They attempted to prevent the German bombers from getting through to drop their bombs on British ports and airfields. To many people at the time, the Spitfire pilots were the heroes of what was known as the "Battle of Britain."

A Spitfire in flight over the green fields of southern England.

FACT FILE

★ The word "spitfire" dates from the reign of Elizabeth I (1558 to 1603) and refers to a fiery, ferocious type of person, usually a woman. The chief designer of the aircraft, R.J. Mitchell, was not impressed, stating that it was the "sort of silly name they would give it."

★ There were 24 different models of Spitfire produced, as well as many variations of those types. The most common was the Mk V, with 6,479 built. In total, 22,789 Spitfires took to the skies between 1938 and 1948, when production ended.

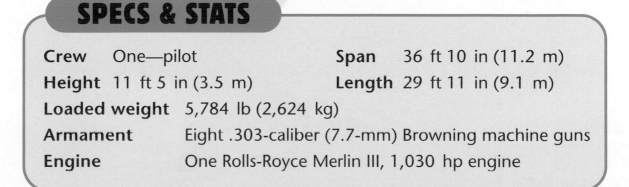

PERFORMANCE

Maximum speed	362 mph (582 km/h)
Range	395 miles (636 km)
Service ceiling	31,900 ft (9,723 m)

▲ *The shape of the Spitfire's wingtips made it instantly recognizable.*

SPECS & STATS

Crew	One—pilot	**Span**	36 ft 10 in (11.2 m)
Height	11 ft 5 in (3.5 m)	**Length**	29 ft 11 in (9.1 m)
Loaded weight	5,784 lb (2,624 kg)		
Armament	Eight .303-caliber (7.7-mm) Browning machine guns		
Engine	One Rolls-Royce Merlin III, 1,030 hp engine		

Douglas
SBD Dauntless

The Douglas SBD Dauntless was the U.S. Navy's main dive bomber in the early years of the war in the Pacific Ocean against Japan.

It was involved in the Pacific war from the start when Dauntlesses from USS *Enterprise* arrived at Pearl Harbor on December 7, 1941, during the Japanese attack.

The Battle of Midway

The most important contribution made by the Dauntless occurred at the Battle of Midway in June 1942. Operating from aircraft carriers and escorted by F4F Wildcat fighters, Dauntlesses sank four Japanese aircraft carriers and heavily damaged two cruisers.

Four Dauntlesses cruise over the Pacific during World War II.

A pair of Dauntlesses prepare for action on the deck of a U.S. aircraft carrier.

FACT FILE

★ A dive bomber dives straight down at its target at high speed and releases its bombs as close to the target as possible. In this way, it avoids some antiaircraft fire and can accurately place its bombs on a relatively small or moving target.

★ From its first delivery in May 1940, 5,936 Dauntlesses were produced, with the last one manufactured on July 21, 1944.

PERFORMANCE

Maximum speed	255 mph (410 km/h)
Range	773 miles (1,244 km)
Service ceiling	25,530 ft (7,780 m)

SPECS & STATS

Crew	Two—pilot, gunner	**Span**	41 ft 6 in (12.65 m)
Height	13 ft 7 in (4.14 m)	**Length**	33 ft 1 in (10.08 m)
Loaded weight	10,676 lb (4,843 kg)		
Armaments	Two .50-caliber (12.7-mm) forward-firing machine guns		
	Two .30-caliber (7.62-mm) flexible-mounted machine guns		
	2,250-lb (1,020-kg) bombs		
Engine	One Wright R-1820-60, radial, 1,200 hp engine		

North American
P-51 Mustang

The North American P–51 Mustang entered military service in 1942 and soon became one of the most successful aircraft of World War II.

The Mustang was a single-seat fighter aircraft and was used to escort bombers when they raided Germany. It also saw service against the Japanese in the Pacific.

The maiden flight of the Mustang took place on October 26, 1940. Although mainly used as a fighter, it was possible to increase its bomb-carrying capacity and turn the aircraft into a useful fighter-bomber.

▼ *The P-51 Mustang was one of the most versatile aircraft of World War II.*

FACT FILE

★ The teardrop-shaped bubble canopy on later models (right) gave the pilot unrestricted vision in all directions.

★ After the war, many Mustangs were converted for civilian use and were particularly well suited for air racing.

SPECS & STATS

Crew	One—pilot	**Span**	37 ft (11.28 m)
Height	13 ft 8 in (4.17 m)	**Length**	32 ft 3 in (9.83 m)

Loaded weight 9,200 lb (4,175 kg)

Armament Six .50-caliber (12.77-mm) machine guns; 400 rounds per gun for the two inboard guns, 270 rounds per outboard gun
Ten 5-in (127-mm) rockets
2,000-lb (907-kg) bombs

Engine One Packard Merlin V-1650-7, liquid-cooled, supercharged, V-12, 1,695 hp engine

◄ *Rows of Mustangs line up on the island of Iwo Jima in the western Pacific.*

▼ *An airplane is being refueled.*

PERFORMANCE

Maximum speed	437 mph (703 km/h) at 25,000 ft (7,620 m)
Cruising speed	362 mph (580 km/h)
Range	1,650 miles (2,655 km) with external fuel tanks
Service ceiling	41,900 ft (12,770 m)

Avro Lancaster

On the night of May 17, 1943, a group of British Avro Lancaster bombers from 617 Squadron carried out the "Dambusters" raid, one of the most famous air raids of World War II.

The Dambusters

The aircraft dropped specially designed bouncing bombs that skimmed across reservoirs before sinking to explode at the base of their targets—the Eder and Möhne dams in the Ruhr valley in Germany. The dams collapsed, sending walls of water through the Ruhr valley and flooding many mines and factories.

▼ *The Avro Lancaster could carry a great weight of bombs.*

The Lancaster was designed as a night bomber, although it was also used for daytime bombing and reconnaissance work. Its 33-ft (10.05-m) long bomb bay allowed it to carry bombs as heavy as 22,000 lbs (9,980 kg).

▲ *The undercarriage needed to be sturdy to support the Lancaster when it landed after a bombing mission.*

FACT FILE

★ The Avro Lancaster made its maiden flight on January 9, 1941 and was introduced into Royal Air Force service the following year. A total of 7,377 aircraft were produced.

★ Lancasters flew 156,000 operations and dropped 681,457 tons (618,380 t) of bombs from 1942 to 1945.

PERFORMANCE

Maximum speed	280 mph (450 km/h) at 15,000 ft (5,600 m)
Cruising speed	200 mph (322 km/h)
Range	2,700 miles (4,300 km) with minimal bomb load
Service ceiling	23,500 ft (8,160 m)

SPECS & STATS

Crew	Seven – pilot, flight engineer, navigator, bombadier, radio operator, mid-upper gunner, rear gunner
Span	102 ft (31.09 m)
Height	19 ft 7 in (5.97 m)
Length	69 ft 5 in (21.18 m)
Loaded weight	63,000 lb (29,000 kg)
Armament	Eight .303 caliber (7.7 mm) Browning machine guns in three turrets 22,000 lb (10,000 kg) bombs, maximum
Engines	Four Rolls-Royce Merlin XX, V-12, 1,280 hp engines

Glossary

Biplane
Aircraft with two parallel wings, one on top of the other.

Bomber
Aircraft designed to carry and drop bombs.

Caliber
Diameter of the bore of a rifle or machine gun, in inches.

Camouflage
Use of paint, material or other substance to conceal the outlines of an aircraft and thus confuse the enemy.

Dive bomber
Aircraft that dives almost vertically to attack its target.

Escort plane
An aircraft accompanying another in order to protect it from enemy attack.

Fighter
Aircraft designed to fight other aircraft.

Fuselage
Main body of an aircraft

hp
Horsepower, a unit of power.

Inline engine
Engine in which the cylinders are in either a single front-to-back row, or in several rows in a 'V' or 'W' shape.

Interceptor
Aircraft designed to attack or prevent an enemy aircraft reaching its target.

Landing gear
Wheels, shock absorbers, struts, and other items that support an aircraft on the ground and enable it to take off and land; also called the undercarriage.

Luftwaffe
The German air force.

Machine gun
Rapid-firing weapon.

Maiden flight
The first-ever flight of an aircraft.

Mk
Short for Mark, the model or type of aircraft.

Monocoque
From the French words *mono* for single and *coque* for eggshell, a construction technique that supports the structural load of the aircraft using its external skin, rather than an internal framework.

Radial engine
Type of aircraft engine with fixed cylinders arranged in a circle around a rotating crankshaft.

Reconnaissance
Obtaining information about the position, activities, resources, and intentions of the enemy; spying

Rotary engine
Type of aircraft engine where the cylinders rotate around a fixed crankshaft.

Seaplane
Aircraft that can take off and land on water using floats rather than wheels.

Service ceiling
The highest an aircraft can safely fly without endangering plane or crew.

Trademark
The legally registered name or symbol of a product that is protected by law against competitors.

Triplane
Aircraft with three parallel wings, on top of each other.

Victoria Cross
British military award for outstanding bravery, first awarded by Queen Victoria in 1856.

Us ful Web Sit s

The Aerodrome-Aces and Aircraft of World War I
www.theaerodrome.com

The Aviation History Online Museum
www.aviation-history.com

The British Imperial War Museum
www.iwm.org.uk

Sites about the two World Wars:

The Great War (World War I) from PBS
www.pbs.org/greatwar/

The Perilous Fight: America's World War II in Color
www.pbs.org/perilousfight/battlefield/

BBC history sites about the two world wars:
www.bbc.co.uk/history/worldwars/wwone/
www.bbc.co.uk/history/worldwars/wwtwo/

Note to Parents and Teachers:
Every effort has been made by the publishers to ensure that the websites in
this book are suitable for children, that they are of the highest educational
value, and that they contain no inappropriate or offensive material.
However, because of the nature of the Internet, it is impossible to
guarantee that the contents of these sites will not be altered. We strongly
advise that Internet access is supervised by a responsible adult.

Index